For SOLANNE, C.M.

For DAVID, DYLAN, CAOLAN and ETHAN, H.R.

Many thanks to the staff and children at
Chalvey Nursery School and Assessment Unit,
and Salt Hill Nursery, Slough, Berkshire
for their help and advice.

Copyright © 2000 Zero to Ten Limited
Text copyright © 1996 Hannah Reidy
Illustrations copyright © 1996 Clare Mackie

Publisher: Anna McQuinn, Art Director: Tim Foster
Art Editor: Sarah Godwin, Designer: Suzy McGrath

First published in Great Britain in hardback in 1996
This edition published in 2000 by Zero to Ten Limited
327 High Street, Slough, Berkshire, SL1 1TX

ISBN 1-84089-070-3
Printed in Hong Kong

Crazy Creatures
Counting

Written by
Hannah Reidy

7 2 6
9 3 2 1
5 8
10 4

Illustrated by
Clare Mackie

One

dim, dippy
creature -
wondering
about
a one.

Two
toothless,
tip-toeing
creatures -
timidly
touching
a two.

Three
careful, calculating creatures - seriously studying a three.

Four
**fabulous,
flashy
creatures -
dizzily
dancing
with
a four.**

Five
hefty,
hairy
creatures -
happily
hugging
a five.

Six
silly, skinny
creatures -
pinkily
kissing
a six.

Seven

swooshing
and
whooshing
creatures -
hustling,
bustling and
skiing down
a seven.

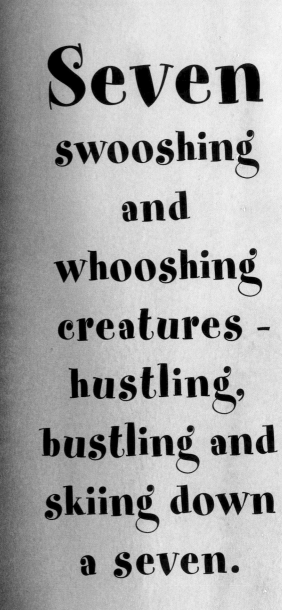

Eight
late, putting-
on-weight
creatures -
lunching,
by munching
and crunching
an eight.

Nine
nice but naughty creatures – slipping and slopping, dripping and dropping their paint on a nine.

Ten
high-kicking
can-can
creatures -
all in a row,
each pointing
a toe,
again and
again,
a chorus-line
ten!

Crazy Creature Concepts

Hannah Reidy and Clare Mackie

"...introducing concepts in an inspiring way."
THE GOOD BOOK GUIDE

Crazy Creatures Counting

"...inspired alliterative text and zany illustrations provide an introduction to numbers and suggest that language can be enormous fun."
TIME OUT

Crazy Creature Colours

"... shows that learning colours need not be a chore."
THE INDEPENDENT

Crazy Creature Capers
Crazy Creature Contrasts

"lively playful text, designed to build concepts of opposites and prepositions, works well to make the learning process enjoyable."
THE SCHOOL LIBRARIAN

Crazy Creature Colours   1-84089-069-X
Crazy Creature Counting   1-84089- 070-3
Crazy Creature Capers   1-84089- 071-1
Crazy Creature Contrasts   1-84089-072-X

In Between Books

Hannah Reidy and Emma Dodd

If you enjoyed the **Crazy Creatures**, you will love these titles, also by Hannah Reidy

"Bridge the gap between first-word books and simple story books..."
JUNIOR MAGAZINE

"... I didn't think it was possible to have a new slant on early counting – but here it is... it's all much too attractive!"
THE GUARDIAN

What do you like to Wear?   1-84089-106-8
What Noises can you Hear?   1-84089-103-3
What does it Look like?   1-84089-104-1
How Many can you See?   1-84089-105-X

ZERO TO TEN books are available from all good bookstores. If you have problems obtaining any title, please contact the publishers:

Zero to Ten Limited
327 High Street, Slough
Berks, SL1 1TX

Tel: 01753 578 499
Fax: 01753 578 488